little
things
make a
big
difference

little
things
make a
big
difference

Laurin Sydney

LIFE
Styles

Hay House, Inc.
Carlsbad, California • Sydney, Australia
Canada • Hong Kong • United Kingdom

Published and distributed in the United States by:
Hay House, Inc., P.O. Box 5100, Carlsbad, CA 92018-5100
(800) 654-5126 • (800) 650-5115 (fax) • www.hayhouse.com
Hay House Australia Pty Ltd, P.O. Box 515, Brighton-Le-Sands,
NSW 2216 • phone: 1800 023 516 • e-mail: info@hayhouse.com.au

Editorial Supervision: Jill Kramer
Cover and Interior Design: Ashley Parsons
Illustrations: Cynthia Allison

Library of Congress Cataloging-in-Publication Data

Sydney, Laurin.
    Little things make a big difference / Laurin Sydney.
        p. cm.
    ISBN 1-56170-951-4 (hardcover)
1. Conduct of life. I. Title.

BF637.C5 S94 2002
158.1—dc21

                                                        2001051473

ISBN 1-56170-951-4

05 04 03 02   4 3 2 1
1st printing, June 2002

Printed in China by Imago

Big Thank Yous!

Not to sound redundant, but little things make a big difference to me, and so do these incredible individuals . . . their spectacular spirits, tireless talents, incredible intellects, and Herculean hearts have guided and glided me through this Hay House experience . . . and through life!

It's with gargantuan gratitude that I thank the following fantastic folks for the creation of this book. (I know, a lot of superlatives, but they deserve it!):

Louise Hay; Reid Tracy; Danny Levin; Jill Kramer; Ashley Parsons; Chandra Teitscheid; Cynthia Allison; Jan Miller; Michael Broussard; Dana Horn; Muffin Gifford; Nicole Von Ruden; Sarah Kraemer; Yvette Mincheff; Jim Moret; Pilar Rossi on Madison Avenue; Johanna Stella of Stella Salon; José Eber; Shelby Meizlick; The Lesser, Einhorn/Sidoti, Locks, Huberman, and Burk clans . . . Lynn, Tiger, Tess, Sid, and "Planey"!

Thank you for making such a big dif to all who know you!

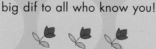

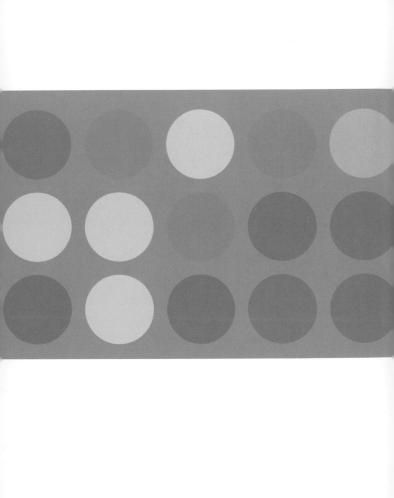

Contents

Was it Napoleon who first said, "Good things come in small packages" . . . or someone in the jewelry industry? Whoever coined that phrase had the wisdom to realize that "little things can make a big difference."

This book is filled with innovative ideas, joyful jolts, and enlightening exercises that will enhance your relationships with your friends, lovers, kids, co-workers . . . and yourself. You'll also learn some ways to enliven your home and workplace—small touches that will change your environment for the better. Now I'm not trying to sound like a Hallmark card; I just want you to realize that just a little effort can go a long way—simple gestures that may not help to establish world peace, but which *can* bring peace and joy to your world . . .

- One little chocolate kiss, added to the lunchbox of a frightened first grader . . .

- A package of dried chicken soup slipped inside of a get-well card for your sniffling sister . . .

- A hanky with your perfume on it, strategically placed in your honey's business luggage . . .

- Some "apple" tea for your daughter's teacher on her birthday . . .

- A sprig of dried lavender slipped into your pillowcase to ensure sweet dreams . . .

- A Band-Aid placed over a child's heart, acknowledging that you know their feelings are hurt . . .

- Placing an image of your favorite peaceful environment on your desk for an instant mental getaway . . .

These are just a few abbreviated examples of some little things that can change a life! . . .

For the past 15 years, as the entertainment anchor for CNN, I've been privy to the private lives of Hollywood royalty, where a wish is their staff's command. Past the tall palms and long driveways of dreams . . . lives a world filled with so much success and privilege that you'd think that *anyone* would be happy. But happiness is not about the grand gesture, not about that house on the hill—it's about constructing a home in your heart. . . .

When Garth Brooks broke the record for the most CDs ever sold, I sent him . . . a broken record. Not the most extravagant present on Earth, but one that he cherishes to this day. When I need-ed to come up with a thank-you gift for a star who shall remain nameless (but who's married to Jennifer Aniston), I wrapped it up in a copy of his last great movie review—boy, did *I* get a great review for this small effort.

Use this book as a guide, and I promise you that in no time you'll be coming up with your own "little things." Every once in a while, you may come across an idea that doesn't seem to be up your alley, but try it, stretch your boundaries, and enlarge your comfort zone . . . it may not be as "little" as you think.

We've already been taught to not sweat the small stuff. *Now* let some small stuff make a big difference for you!

Little Things for

So many times in my life, I've wished that I could wiggle my nose and become two people. One Laurin would wake up, work out, shower, clog her pores with TV makeup, work her tush off, pick up the check, and come home . . . while the other Laurin would wake up and spend the entire day nurturing relationships and just doing the right thing. But since the "Samantha" trick really only works in TV-rerun heaven, we're all left with the problem of not having enough time to do the things we *want* to do.

Our days become divided into the "want tos and have tos." I want to buy a little present for my daughter's teacher, but I have to go to the office. I want to catch up with some college friends, but I have to take my precious pup, Malibu, to the vet. (Don't worry; I'm not going to bore you with more frustrating examples!) But no matter how we reshuffle our days, we never seem to have enough time for the "want tos." What sometimes happens is that people tend to shut down completely without even making an attempt at a scaled-down version of their "want tos." They figure that if they can't do the whole kit-and-caboodle, they won't do anything! But here are a bunch of little things to the rescue . . . small ideas that cast a long ray of sunshine.

Couldn't Be Better

Ask Tom Hanks any day of the week, "How ya doin'?" and invariably you'll receive "Couldn't be better" as the response. True, Tom has a fantastic wife, fabulous kids, a phenomenal career, and is adored by zillions, but even during his down times, his answer will always be upbeat. Hopeful, happy words make a big difference, so sprinkle your vocabulary with superlatives, and they'll serve as a positive affirmation.

Wow! This was a brilliant, stupendous, miraculous, awesome, spectacular, fantabulous, splendiferous idea!

The Dream Machine

A CNN producer once told the wonderful Katie Couric that she'd never make it in television . . . High school coaches thought that Michael Jordan wasn't good enough to make the basketball team . . . and Barbra Streisand was warned that her nose would sniff out all hopes of her becoming a star. But all three had dreams that were too strong to be shattered by negativity.

I grew up thinking that I could become the first female president because I had parents who constantly encouraged my pie-in-the-sky attitude. I would randomly receive little notes from my mom, encouraging life on the other side of "the glass ceiling." In my dad's eyes, I was an Olympic gold medal gymnast, even though I could barely do a handstand.

So be a dream promoter to those around you. Little words of encouragement help float big ideas. Walt Disney was once told by a teacher to stop dreaming. What if he had listened?!

Strangers in Paradise

Take the time to tell a stranger what a great job they did! A receptionist, a telephone operator, a train conductor, a busboy, a crossing guard . . . we all need a little boost.

Get-Well Wonders

Your friend is sick and there's no time in your busy schedule to make Grandma's chicken soup from scratch! Hey, whatever happened to, "It's the thought that counts"? Call a deli near your favorite "patient's" home, pay by credit card, and have the soup delivered. If there's no deli, then wonton or miso soup will do. And if you're planning on sending a get-well card, slip a package of dried chicken soup in the envelope, or seal it with a Band-Aid.

Flower Power

I often wonder whether the world would be a better place if Adam had given Eve a lush bouquet of fragrant flowers! The power of flowers is unending. We use them to romance, to apologize, to create an atmosphere, and to cajole. But sometimes when you need to count on "Mother Nature's Magical Miracles," you just may not have the time, convenience, or money to procure some powerful petals. Don't give up just because you can't go for the grand gesture . . . you can always use a substitute! A flowered tie, gardenia-scented stationery, a bunch of dried lavender, or even a CD of "Tiptoe Through the Tulips" will get your point across.

And in an SOS situation, when you want to give someone flowers even though there isn't a florist (or extra time) available, just quickly open any magazine. Do a quick flip of the pages and you'll come up with a *picture* of some flowers. Present that with your written words . . . and the memory will never wilt!

Ring-a-Ling-a-Ling

No matter what her happy meter is at any given moment, my soon-to-be mother-in-law always answers the phone as if Clark Gable is on the other end. She has the most inviting hello that translates into, "Hi, I know who it is, and I'm thrilled that you called!" Her warm, inviting beginning to the call ensures a great middle and an equally great end.

No matter what the circumstances are around you, try to bring new energy to each call. Whether it's personal or professional, that split-second welcome sets the entire tone.

Pass on a "Wow"

It's so joyous to watch little kids say the word *Wow!* So many tiny miracles cross our paths on the road to *Wow.* Then we grow up, and the wows are few and far between . . . but oh-so-special when they arrive. So now, instead of sending jokes over the Internet, I've gotten in the habit of passing on the *Wow,* kind of like a chain letter of amazing moments. The next time you say it, share it . . . there just aren't enough of them anymore.

Thanx

Sometimes the right thank-you note can be even more memorable than the gift that was given. Whether you had the time of your life or were so bored that you fell asleep behind your menu, there is always a creative way to say thank you.

For instance:

- Take a pack of matches from the restaurant where you ate, and tell your host that the evening was "unmatchable."

- Add a little "prop" to your note. If someone did you a huge favor, put in a pack of Lifesavers, telling them that they were your . . . you guessed it! For affection, add a chocolate kiss . . . for a celebration, some confetti . . . and for relaxation, a sprig of dried lavender.

- If you were invited to a great tennis match, write your thank-you note on a tennis ball.

- If you had dinner at the home of a friend who collected china monkeys, write the note on a banana (I know you're rolling your eyes), but I did this for a well-known celeb and received a thank you for my thank you.

Just be personal, have fun with your ideas, and go for it. Creativity doesn't require artistic ability . . . just the ability to stretch the limits that bind us.

Sugar-Coated Memories

Sights, sounds, smells, and tastes can take us back in time instantly. As a little treat, I sometimes go down memory lane with a "retro-snack," sending all of my college friends our junk food of choice, which fueled our long evenings of studying.

To my camp buddies, it's the little sugar dots on paper that are so bad for your teeth . . . but so much fun to scarf down! At first, when I started to send these sweet sensations, I didn't even know where to find my childhood candy. I thought they might be petrified in the Museum of Natural History (just a little self-deprecating humor)! But I was surprised to find that everything old is new again. Some of my favorite tastes are in updated and improved packaging . . . little sweet memories of yesterday . . . when all our cellulite seemed so far away!

It Was a Very Good Year

Even if you're not a drinker, for birthdays and anniversary gifts, your local liquor store is the place to go. Buy an old bottle of wine whose year corresponds with the one you want to celebrate. The date a couple got married, the year Aunt Tillie was born . . . okay, even if milk is on the menu, buy a bottle of champagne for a newborn, with the understanding that they pop the cork on their 21st birthday!

Family Ties

The great thing about home video cameras is that they not only record baby's first step, but they also act as the historian for the family. The camera is there for all the school plays, the championship soccer matches, and Granny's 70th birthday party. But so much of our family "love" slips through the cracks due to a lack of the written word. It's normal for us to keep personal journals, but the family's story always seems to take a backseat to our own life story. From now on, alternate being the secretary of the family, contributing to a journal that tells *everyone's* story. Let your little ones take part in this ritual as soon as they can communicate. It's so priceless to watch their simple pictures turn into prose.

Turn a Pity Party into a Pamper Party

You and a friend are sitting around wallowing in negativity when your pity patience button goes off and you realize that enough is enough. Negative energy is only good for batteries. So pick yourself up and turn your pity party into a pamper party. If you don't have enough green stuff to go to a local day spa, seek out a beauty school in your area for inexpensive indulgence.

These schools often set aside certain times of the week when they offer their services free to the public for training purposes. I don't think I would necessarily let them perm my eye lashes, but the price is definitely right for facials, massages, and pedicures. And if there's no beauty school in your 'hood, then you and your friend can pamper one another. Just take turns polishing, shining, and generally caring for each other.

Life's Lovely Little Leftovers

We think nothing of reheating that dry slice of pepperoni pizza . . . so why not reheat memories? On my Daddy's birthday every year, the time I miss him the most, I bring together a group of folks who knew him best. We spend the night telling delicious "Sid Stories," warming the memories in our hearts. I try to invite different sets of people, always hoping to elicit new shreds of information. I've been doing this now for about 12 years, and it's so interesting to see how the stories evolve. Facts get inflated and circumstances get exaggerated, just adding to a life . . . that was bigger than life.

Remember, if you don't use it, you lose it . . . so keep those memories sharp and present by reheating them constantly.

Sealed
with a
Kiss

Slipping an unexpected Hershey's Kiss into an eyeglass case, briefcase, or pocketbook, can give your loved one a joyful jolt. (But you'd better not do it if the air conditioner's on the blink—you don't want any chocolate meltdowns!)

Just in case chocolate doesn't float your boat, a little note will do the trick . . . or even a small picture—any unexpected little treat. When Julia Roberts won an Oscar for *Erin Brockovich,* her hotel suite resembled a luxurious floral shop. Magnificent arrangements were coming in by the dozens, each one more exquisite than the next. But it was the simple gesture made by her then-boyfriend Benjamin Bratt that stole her heart. He ripped off a corner of the Oscar program and wrote a note saying how proud of her he was and slipped it into her pocketbook while she was doing the obligatory press interviews.

You see, Julia knows that little things make a big difference.

Silent Night

When Christmas is over, I always feel an emptiness. It's partly because the family has gone home, the mistletoe has come down, and it's truly a silent night because all of the beautiful holiday music gets put away for at least 326 days. It's kind of like only having turkey with the trimmings on Thanksgiving. I love to play Christmas music all year long. There's nothing like hearing "Frosty the Snowman" on a hot, steamy summer day. Play "The Christmas Song (Chestnuts Roasting on an Open Fire")" at a cocktail party and watch the expression on guests' faces change. Of course, as with everything else, don't overdo it or it will lose its charm.

Kiss 'n' Tell

You've spent all day in the mall shopping for the perfect present, you plop down on the couch to soothe your aching feet and wrap your masterpiece . . . when the truth unveils itself. You have no ribbon, no wrapping paper . . . just an ugly, beat-up box. Time to race to the store . . . but no, you don't want to—you've been running around all day.

Well, all you have to do is run over to your makeup drawer and pick out the reddest lipstick of the bunch. Generously put it on your lips and start smooching the box on the top and sides so that your lip prints are about an inch away from each other . . . if you're a guy, no one's going to kiss 'n' tell! Either borrow a pair of lips, go to the store . . . or go for it!

And if lips aren't appropriate on a gift for your daughter's school principal, just get out your trusty marker and write the person's name repeatedly all over the box. You don't need good handwriting—you just need good wishes. You can also write meaningful phrases on the box, such as "Your friendship means a lot to me," or practical ones, such as "You have until May 6th to return this!"

Complimentary Compliments

I could be wrong, but I don't think Meg Ryan really needs to hear one more time that she has a trillion-dollar smile. But recently, when I told a waitress that *she* had a lovely smile, I was so touched by her response. With tears in her eyes, she handed me the check and told me that no one in her life had ever given her a compliment before. Of course, at that point I wanted to sign over the deed to my house as a tip! She went on to say that she would remember the moment forever.

The power of a genuine compliment is immense. I know that your mom taught you to find the good in everything . . . so when you do find it, speak up! It's free, and the impact can be miraculous.

In Focus

So many unusual things have happened to me while talking to celebrities live on television. Aside from the scenery falling down and a "married" star attempting to play footsie with me under the desk, every once in a while I learn an interesting life lesson. Once, during an interview, a superstar (who shall remain nameless because she doesn't want anyone to know she's over 40) was cleaning her reading glasses. When she was finished, she reached over and started cleaning mine. A tad unusual, I thought, but then she went on to explain that in France, this is a normal custom, serving to pass on clarity of vision and spirit. I now pass this on to you!

Golden
Reminders

The Golden Door, a fantastic, phenomenal, fabulous spa in Escondido, California (can you tell I like it there?!), not only pampers your body, it also pampers your soul. Beneath the eucalyptus trees and serene koi ponds, they've instituted a gentle way to reinforce your goals. After a discussion about your hopes for the future, they have you write down anything you want to accomplish in the coming year and place it in a self-addressed stamped envelope. Then you have someone in your group hold on to these letters and mail them back to you at a random time. One day, when you're not expecting it, you receive the envelope in your mailbox. If you've accomplished your goal, good for you! If not, this quiet reminder gives you the impetus to keep on truckin'.

You'll get there. It's your life's timetable.

Double Your Pleasure

Okay, this might be one of those ideas that isn't in your comfort zone, but I encourage you to try it just once. This is such a hoot—I can guarantee tons of smiles, lots of new acquaintances, and interesting conversations. All you have to do is play dress-up! That's right—plan to dress up like twins with a really good friend. You'll be amazed at how many new people you meet with just minimal effort.

Good Tears

For me, it's *It's a Wonderful Life*; for my honey, it's *Young Man with a Horn*. Every once in a while (when you're wearing waterproof mascara), it's cathartic to pile on to the couch with a box of tissues and your good buddies, and watch your favorite tearjerker. Not only does it sharpen your emotions, but it also helps you remember how lucky you are.

Good tears also provide an outlet for pent-up emotions, which is why you always feel better after a good cry!

Creative Cakes

Okay, so you forgot someone's birthday, and now it's too late to rustle up a cake because the bakeries are closed. Have no fear—cupcakes are here! Just go to your local grocery store and pick up some of those sweet little concoctions. If you're so inclined, then make them yourself! Now, arrange the cupcakes on the kitchen table so that they're in the configuration of your loved one's age or initials. This is a fresh take on a cake . . . and only *you* will know the secret!

Life Is a Picnic

So, when you went to bed, the guy on the radio said the weather would be sunny and clear the next day. . . . (I used to be a weather fore caster—and take it from the horse's mouth, we're not always right.)

Now, here it is, the morning of the big beach picnic. The cooking's done, the car's packed, and the alarm has just gone off. But you didn't really need the alarm because the thunder and lightning storm has already jolted you out of bed. You go downstairs to some very disappointed faces . . . and you exclaim that the beach picnic is still on!

"I want to see everyone in their swimsuits and sunscreen in 30 minutes . . . and meet me in . . . the living room!"

That's right—you're going to spread your red-and-white checkered tablecloth across your living room floor, lay out all the food and drinks . . . and picnic on, dudes! If you can also play some tunes with the sounds of the ocean (or anything by The Beach Boys), you'll do swimmingly well!

Little Things for *You*

Besides telling us that there aren't any more honey-roasted peanuts left, and reminding us that our tray tables need to be in their upright and locked positions before take-off, flight attendants also instruct us to place the oxygen mask on ourselves before our children in case an emergency arises.

On land, we can also deal with others more effectively if we take care of ourselves first. Now, I'm not advocating running out to get a pedicure while your kids are stranded on the playground, but so many of us feel that stinging twinge of guilt when we try to enhance our own lives. But somewhere on the road between selfish and selfless lives a place where your strength and joy can radiate out to everyone around you. Use the following luscious little ideas . . . and start radiating!

Romance for One, Please!

I promise you, this is not kinky! How many times have you bought that silk nightie, scented candles, and a brand-new jazz CD for that special someone, only to find out that months later, you don't even want to hear their name? Well, the good news is that *you're* the special someone. Please don't deprive yourself of living a romantic life because you don't have a partner! Sure, if given the choice, I'd take "being madly in love" any day, but until that day, light those candles, sing along with Ella, and have sweet dreams beneath 250-count sheets!

Your Presents Are Required

So there you are on a typical Saturday afternoon. You grab a bite and head to the mall. And then you see that little blue number that you've had your eye on for a while. You think about it, give in, and whip out your credit card. Then there's always that moment when the sales clerk asks, "Shall I wrap it?" and you say, "Nah, it's only for me. . . ."

Well, what's wrong with a little icing on your cake? Next time, wrap it up and then open it later like it's a gift . . . from you . . . to you!

Blast from the Past

Dust off an old phone-book and call someone meaningful from your past. If "I'm sorry, this number is no longer in service" greets you at the other end, search for the new number at the Website **www.switchboard.com**.

Birthday Bonanza

rinkles aside, try to live every day as if it were your birthday—not because you'll get presents, but because your daily "presence" will change. On our birthdays, we tend to be more open to people's kindness and silently accept the fact that good things will come our way.

In another life, I did TV commercials. I was queen of the ladies' room, representing Tidy Bowl, Lysol, Charmin, Comet, and Close-Up toothpaste. It was a highly competitive world, where the odds were against you, but every year on my birthday, I would audition for, and be cast in, a commercial. Now this wasn't a present given to me by the advertising agency . . . it was the birthday bonanza attitude that I was putting out there that got me the part. So, celebrate every day—you never know what wonderful things might be in store for you!

Lose Blues

Have you ever noticed that you seem to lose stuff in stages? It could be a momentary lack of focus or just too much going on in your life . . . but when your glasses, keys, and other often-used objects start to disappear, you'll find that if you tie a colorful scarf to these items, you'll find them instantly. Warning: This method won't work with your eight-year-old!

If I Had All the Money in the World . . .

Of course I would take care of world hunger and try to eradicate all devastating diseases, but I would also continue a "little thing" I do now. When the mood strikes, I pay for the stranger in the car behind me at the toll booth. In my rearview mirror, I often witness the puzzled expression on the driver's face, reminding me that we shouldn't question kindness, but just accept it, however it comes.

Say "Cheese"!

I'm not trying to raise your cholesterol—I'm trying to raise your spirits! This is one of those ideas that you might read over a couple of times and decide to skip because you think it would make you feel self-conscious . . . but it will also make you feel really good. Give it a chance, since you have nothing to lose.

Here it is: Just smile at yourself in the mirror every day (no, not to see if you have lettuce in your teeth)—but to establish a good mood for the day!

Grateful Grocery List

Many times when I'm jottin' down milk, juice, and eggs on one list, I take another piece of paper, date it, and jot down what I'm grateful for at that very second! I stuff it in a pocket, change purse, or in a back drawer, where it will live until the day it makes a surprise guest appearance. It's amazing how I always seem to find these little bits of paper when I need them most!

Lollipop Theory

Remember when you were a kid, how you went to the dentist to have a cavity filled and then got a lollipop on the way out? I never quite understood why dentists handed out sugar on a stick, but maybe it was to ensure repeat business! In any case, the idea of receiving a little treat after you've accomplished a goal is a great idea and one that I practice on a daily basis. Anytime I have to do something that's not my favorite task, I put the lollipop theory into play. The little treat doesn't have to be food, but it should always be something you really like. Here are some of my quick picks:

- After I weed my garden, only then can I cut and arrange my roses.

- After I clean my desktop, I can snuggle up and read some of my favorite letters from my special drawer.

- After I clean, peel, and chop all the vegetables for the soup, I can ice the cake (and sample the icing!).

Customize the method that works for your own likes and dislikes and you'll see how easily you'll accomplish what usually gets put off for a while. And guess what? They have delicious sugarless lollys now!

Rain, Rain, Go Away

I know you've all heard of dressing for success . . . well, what about dressing for happiness? Why should dismal weather rule our attitudes? On the darkest, dankest, dampest day, I pull out my pale pinks and uplifting azure blues to raise my personal barometer. I'm not sure wearing a bikini in a blizzard is a great idea, but don't allow Mother Nature to be your wardrobe consultant. Not only will you be lifting your own spirits, but everyone around you will also be affected.

Zeeeeeee's

Ze important element to clarity, creativity, and productivity is energy. When our batteries are run down, so are our efforts. Sometimes, just a 15-minute catnap can refresh our energy . . . but too many of us feel this odd guilt over the need to replenish ourselves. Give yourself permission to catch a few z's. Specify a certain place, pillow, and throw as your napping tools. And then when you awaken, a little milk and cookies (or soy milk and Snackwells) will set you on your way.

Puppy Love

Oh, poop—your apartment complex doesn't allow you to have pets. Oh, poop—your mother-in-law is allergic to cats. If you get one, there goes the free baby-sitting service. Oh, poop—for some reason or other, that precious puppy that stared at you (and only you) from the pet shop window won't be coming home with you this time. But that doesn't mean you can't have pets in your life.

I'm not advising that you go out and get a goldfish named Rover . . . I'm simply suggesting that you visit your local pet store or animal shelter regularly. It's been medically proven that petting animals can substantially lower your blood pressure and release endorphins, which boost your immune system. You could also cat-sit for your neighbors when they're on vacation, take their dogs out for a little stroll, or offer to brush Fluffy the cat's coat a few times a week.

So don't be embarrassed. Add those trips to the pet store, shelter, or your neighbor's home to your schedule . . . and pet away. Your new furry friends will be most appreciative!

Your Own Personal Fan Club!

Yes, we are all created equal—except that celebrities employ a staff to remind them how divine they actually are. Now, just in case your staff is on a permanent vacation, remind yourself what a good job you've been doing. Literally take a moment and pat yourself on the back. You don't need a Greek chorus to recognize your accomplishments—you have *you!*

And while you're patting yourself on the back, don't turn your back on the company you keep. Be sure to associate with people who support you and offer you verbal pats. I once had a friend (notice the word *had*), and every time I saw her, I would come away feeling down for some reason. I suppose she meant well, but she'd say things like, "You're looking a little tired tonight—are we the same age?" Or how about this gem: "You're looking a little puffy. Did you *want* to gain weight?" Harmless comments, but who needs them?! We're entitled to choose our friends, so make a point of hanging out with members of your own fan club.

Soundtrack of Your Life

I t's not unusual to share a song with your honey, and when it randomly plays on the radio, time just seems to stand still! But what about that song that means so much to you that every time you hear it, it brings goose bumps to your spine and a smile to your soul? Keep that song handy, and play it as if it's dessert. It can physically energize you or magically relax you. It's *yours*.

You're Never Alone

Due to the way the bus route ran, as a three-year-old, I was always the last kid to be dropped off from day care. But Mom taught me that I was never really alone. Whenever I started to feel my little lower lip quiver, she reminded me to hold my own hand for company—and to this day, whenever I really miss her and reach out to hold her hand, I hold my own.

I've even reached for this "handful" of a security blanket while broadcasting live on the air. During a particularly difficult assignment, when news was breaking all over the place, my earpiece connecting me to the control room and producer broke . . . leaving me without a way to get information and feeling very alone. While people were watching from all over the world, I gently held my own hands and then . . . I proposed to myself . . . just kidding! But really, this gesture made me feel secure. It takes a while to get into this habit, but once you do, you'll never feel alone.

Solo Sunsets

Many years ago, I was in Malibu witnessing the most dazzling sunset I've ever seen. An older gentleman commented on the tears in my eyes and asked me if I often cried when I witnessed great beauty! For some reason, I opened up to this stranger and told him that I was shedding tears because I wished I could have had a man in my life to share this moment with. This kind soul took my hands and said, "You're sharing this with yourself. Don't block the miracle." I was forever changed—and grateful.

Anxiety Insurance

Stuff happens . . . your flight gets delayed . . . the milk has gone sour for your morning coffee . . . you lose your keys. . . . After years of being around some sensational TV producers, I've learned that what makes their unpredictable lives run so smoothly is that they're prepared for every "what if." Now that doesn't mean they're constantly looking for the negative—it simply means they know how to quickly turn a negative into a positive by thinking a step ahead.

So, if your flight gets delayed, whip out the thank-you notes you've been meaning to send for six weeks. Maybe your keys are lost for the moment, but you've already hidden a spare under the fourth rock on your porch . . . and by the way, you *can* freeze milk. Who knew?

Photographic Memory

Hollywood stylists leave nothing to chance when dressing their superstar clients. Once they've achieved a look that they want to capture again, they lay out the clothes and accessories and snap a picture. You may not need to use this method for your next PTA meeting, but it will definitely save you valuable time on a groggy morning as you try to figure out what scarf goes with which suit for that important meeting.

The Big "Turn-Off"

We might fill up the tank and drive a couple of hours to the mountains to hear the birds chirp and the wind blow through the pines . . . but all of these delicious sounds might be right in your own backyard! It's difficult to hear the crickets at night when you're being lulled to sleep by Letterman's top-ten list. Tonight, turn it all off—the whirring fan, the ticking clock, the humming fax machine . . . and just listen. Not only will you be surprised by what you hear, but you'll also save on gas!

Trading Places

Every day, as I walk around my New York neighborhood, I see individuals who seem to have the weight of the world on their shoulders. So, when I suffer a disappointment, I try to focus on the positive aspects of my life. It's important that we remember how lucky we really are despite the challenges that we may be facing at any given time.

Whenever you're feeling sorry for yourself, ask yourself if you would honestly want to trade *your* set of problems for someone else's . . . you'll probably conclude that you're fortunate to be you!

Walking
on Sunshine

I've attended about 46,371 movie premieres in my career (give or take 371 or so). And the thing that I find so astounding (besides the fact that the force of gravity never seems to affect celebrities) is how these Hollywood folks can glide up and down the red carpet in four-inch heels without even a whimper.

They're acting, I initially thought, but then I did a little investigative journalism and uncovered the answer—a simple solution that can put a bounce in your step for a one-time charge of about six dollars. And now, even if I'm wearing four-inch spike heels at a big Hollywood premiere, I always feel as if I'm walking on sunshine.

The thing to do is . . . buy your shoes half a size larger, and insert two Dr. Scholl's pads as insoles. I guarantee you that your hairdo will fade before your footsies will!

Palm Pilot Persuasion

You spend so much time making sure your schedule allows you to take care of all of your professional and domestic needs. Well, if the dog groomer, carpet cleaner, and your mother-in-law all deserve a slot on your busy schedule, what about *you*? Make appointments with yourself and keep them. Carve out time to just do nothing, and you'll be amazed by how rewarding it can be.

Routine
Rituals

When my fantastic sister, Lynn, was uprooted and had to move from Florida to California, knowing no one (except her loving husband), she established a simple ritual that helped to make her feel grounded. Every morning, she fixed herself a breakfast tray with her fancy-schmancy china and a bud vase filled with one flower. With all of the uncertainty inherent in her new life, this morning mantra became a constant in an uncertain world. Whatever your personal preference may be—whether it's daily meditation, a jog on the beach at sunset, or even singing in the shower, it's so important to maintain these little rituals for a sense of stability.

$5 Makeover

Some of my favorite morning television segments involve "magical makeovers," whereby a willing "guinea pig" is transformed from a moth into a butterfly—as open-mouthed friends and family members look on in disbelief. But what isn't shown is how much it costs to have all those high-falutin' magicians applying their make-up tricks, designer fashions, and $250 haircuts.

Well, in your own life, you don't have to break the bank for a new you. A luscious new lip gloss, a silky body lotion, a pair of exotic earrings, lacy panties (it's amazing what they can do with polyester these days!)—and you're set. Items under five dollars don't hurt the pocketbook, but they can give you that special glow! (Of course, the greatest glow comes from within . . . and that costs you nothing!)

Happy You Year!

For the millennium celebration, CNN sent correspondents all over the world to usher in the new century. While my co-host was sent to the Egyptian pyramids, I was stationed in the entertainment capital of the world—Las Vegas. Naturally, we were all dealing with a lot of excitement and revelry, but unfortunately, we also had to deal with the threat of terrorists. Thank goodness there was peace on Earth that night, but while I was broadcasting live, I had no idea what the outcome would be. So when it came time to make my usual New Year's resolution, my cellulite seemed so unimportant. In that split second, I decided that instead of making (and breaking) resolutions, I would gently accept the fact that I will never ever look like Heather Graham. From that point on, I resolved to accept my shortcomings. That doesn't mean I've given myself permission to pig out and exercise by hittin' the ol' remote control . . . I simply gave myself permission to go gently into the New Year.

Have I Got a Tip for You!

A dollar or two spent on unexpected tips can garner million-dollar thank yous. I love to show my appreciation to gas-station attendants, toll-booth takers, train conductors . . . folks who usually don't receive gratuities. You would think I paid for their kid's college education judging by the reception!

Design Your Delete Buttons

What a sense of accomplishment you feel when you push the delete button on your computer and zap away all of those unwanted, unnecessary e-mails. What an even better feeling to do it in your own head. When I'm feeling overwhelmed by all the unnecessary information in my brain, I clear the clutter by deleting what I don't need. Don't hold on to the junk—it leaves less room for the good stuff.

Ready for Your Dreams!

I know you can't remember being 11 months old, but at *that* tender age, your goal wasn't to build up a substantial 401K—it was simply to walk on your own. And you had to start with baby steps—there wasn't any shortcut you could take. Even Fred Astaire and Ricky Martin didn't start out trippin' the light fantastic.

So don't negate the baby steps when you're trying to fulfill your dreams. On your journey, you may wobble and fall on your tush, but those baby steps will add up to a sensational stride.

H₂O
Woe

When things aren't going well for us, we not only feel weighed down mentally, but physically as well. Our energy starts to wear down, and we begin to feel heavy-hearted, as if the weight of the world is on our shoulders. Of course it would be terrific if we could just pick ourselves up, dust ourselves off, and start all over again, but sometimes that only works with song lyrics.

However, a good way to vent some of the frustration you may be feeling is to get in the shower and visualize the water washing your troubles down the drain. It may seem a little bit simplistic, but visualization is a terrific tool—and it works!

The Eyes Have It

I have my Daddy's eyes. I haven't seen his (in person) in over a decade since he went to heaven, but in a way, I gaze at them every single day. In the morning, when I'm applying mascara in a magnifying mirror, it's as if I'm looking at him. Now, I don't want this to sound ghoulish, because it actually warms my heart and soul on a daily basis. It keeps the connection crisp, with all of my wonderful memories in the forefront. I even say "Good morning, Daddy," every A.M. For you, it may be your hands or your voice or even your belly laugh that reminds you of that special someone. Whatever that connection is, hold on to it tightly, cherish it, and celebrate the generation gap.

Be Your Own Scriptwriter

If your life were a movie, how would you characterize it? No, I don't mean R or PG-13 . . . that's none of my business. For instance, mine would be a sensitive musical comedy (even though I know that musicals don't make money anymore!). But honestly, think about which genre describes your life . . . a fantasy, tearjerker, cartoon, heavy drama, mystery, film noir, or a light and breezy romance? Once you've come up with your category, ask yourself if that is the film type you actually want for yourself. Whip out the popcorn if it's not. March straight to the mirror and take a good look at the chief scriptwriter. It's not positive or negative circumstances that define your storyline; it's the context in which you handle them. What becomes melodrama for one person can be rewritten as adventure for another. Life is your blank piece of paper to fill with any script that you choose. So choose wisely!

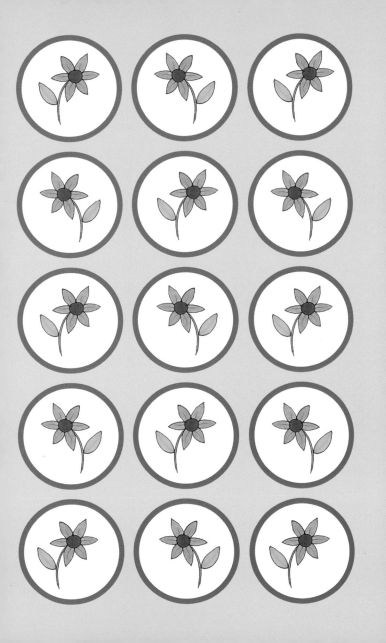

Little Things for

Kids

I don't mean to be bossy, but close your eyes and quickly bring up a couple of your warmest childhood memories. I bet ya dollars to two Krispy Kreme doughnuts that what you remembered involved small details.

It might have been the way Aunt Tessie used to give you two M&M's every time you ran a fever. Or the way the tooth fairy (who always seemed to wear Mom's perfume) left you a crisp dollar bill with your initials on it. Or those personal-pizza nights where your brothers and sisters concocted any combination of toppings that their bellies could tolerate.

My stomach still aches today when I think back to what we actually ate! But after you digest your memories, you'll realize that happy childhoods are made up of moments—those loving rituals that eventually turn into traditions.

Well, here are some more itty-bitty ideas, formulated exclusively for all the itty-bitty people you love—whose own childhood memories you'd like to make delicious. But here's a warning: Think twice before you offer up the personal pizza party—it can become habit-forming!

Penny for Your Thoughts

In this economy, the next time you think that pennies aren't worth anything, think again. Check out the dates on those copper circles because I know that one of them must correspond to the year that a special child in your life was born. Collect these pennies, and insert them in birthday cards as a special remembrance.

Lights Out

Every now and then, have a "before-Thomas Edison evening." No TV, no computer, no lights, no phone—just candlelight conversation with the whole family. It's a good idea to set up sleeping bags in the living room for everybody so that the kids won't be left alone with the lit candles.

Hey, get back in that sleeping bag—no e-mail checking is allowed!

Half-Birthday Bonanza

I'm from the school of thought that every day is a celebration, especially birthdays! So why not celebrate midyear extravaganzas, too? A "half of a cake" on a half-birthday is such a fun way to mark the passage of time—and it's half the calories, right?

Put a Happy Face on Happy Feet

Before a bath, at the beach, or just as a treat for finishing their brussels sprouts, draw a happy face on the bottom fleshy part of your cherub's little toes. It's amazing how this simple work of art can garner a gaggle of giggles. And if you're so inspired, draw one on your own big toe to complete the set!

Don't Cry Over Spilled Milk

In the age-old battle of trying to get your kids to drink milk, it pays to be a square. Simply take your ice tray and fill it three-quarters of the way with chocolate milk. Add a couple of cubes to your regular milk and watch it all disappear. You can also reverse this method by using chocolate milk with white milk cubes. Of course it's a gimmick, but it will work (at least for a couple of years).

Now, I've never met a little cherub who didn't care for juice, and this ice-cube method also works in what I call "wacky water." Fill a large clear pitcher with water, then add different colors and flavors of juice cubes. Your kids will think it's floating magic.

Color My World

Since there's no post office in heaven, and my mommy can't write me any more letters, I often think about the wonderful, warm feeling that I would get if I could just see her handwriting on an envelope again.

But at least I have the memories of being an eight-year-old at Camp Robindel, waiting for mail call. And there it was—an envelope addressed to me in crayon! What a fun thing! When writing a note to one of your little people, why not try using a crayon. The best part is, you don't have to stay in the lines!

Star
Stories

No, I'm not encouraging gossip night—I'm talking about celestial celebs. On a clear, starry night, lie down with your family on a blanket in your backyard. Focus on one star and take turns creating a story around it. When you run out of ideas, switch to another one of nature's shining lights. Sometimes the sandman comes before the show is over!

Lunchbox Bonus

I f I ever found a Twinkie in the lunch I take to work, I would do a jig! As you grow up (and are on TV, where the camera adds 15 pounds), your lunchbox treat becomes an Altoid! Now that I've found The Zone diet, I no longer need any treats, but when you're little, still immersed in the world of Gummi Bears and Starbursts, it's always special to have the "sweetest" treats come from Mom.

So, every day, add a special message to your little one's lunchbox. It could be something you've jotted on a napkin, a sticker placed on a sandwich bag, or a photo that will make your child smile. Some extra-special love nutrition is always a good thing!

Hello, Dolly

You know, there was a time in your life when your stuffed animals and dolls were as lifelike to you as your older sister (and not because she was constantly pulling your hair!). The same is true for your own kids.

In order to honor that notion, plan a tea party, a luncheon, or a dinner where the whole family is invited—and I mean the *whole* menagerie. Set place settings for your kids' primary dolls and animals. Offer them fun food, call them by name, and include these special guests in your conversation. What a magical meal!

Developing Disposable Dreams

It's been raining for 13 days and you've exhausted every single indoor plan known to parenthood. Okay, before all your hair goes gray, give each child a disposable camera and a quick lesson in photography. Using your home as the setting, let each of them shoot a film with a story in mind. Develop the film (at the inexpensive one-hour photo lab), and give the pix back to each budding storyteller with lots of paper, pens, and tape. Have them create a story using every single picture. If your young directors can't write yet, they can tell their stories verbally. A picture-perfect afternoon!

Shapely Snacks

Cookie cutters are not only for cookies! For breakfast, you can pour pancake batter into any shaped metal mold. Dinosaur blueberry pancakes are always a popular item. For lunch, what about a cowboy boot-shaped tuna sandwich? Just press the shape into your bread and discard the remnants outside the mold. You can even use little molds for carrots and celery, but I'm afraid that spinach will always look like spinach.

Cone Heads

One of my best flea-market finds was an old ice cream cone holder I got for 50 cents! I love it so much that I use it all the time—but not for scoops of ice cream or nonfat yogurt. I use it for scoops of anything! Tuna, egg salad, crabmeat salad, cottage cheese, salmon salad, even Jell-O—just scoop the scoopable item and place it on a whole-wheat cone. Your kids will hardly know it's not ice cream! Okay, a little exaggeration, but they'll love this.

Ketchup and Mustard Masterpieces

Pour ketchup and mustard separately into two plastic pointed bottles and just squeeze away. You can make happy faces on a hamburger, flowers on frankfurters, or even write personal messages on the plates around the food. Anything from "Happy birthday, Harry," to "No dessert until you eat your veggies!" It's a squiggly type of nutritional bribe.

Chalk Walk

If you're an apartment dweller, you may have to skip this one, but if you have your own home, this idea will make your kids skip! Using thick, colorful chalk, leave a message or a picture on your front step to welcome your little ones home from school. You don't need to be artistic. A stick figure will do. Even if you're reminding your son about his book report, it's a welcoming way to do it.

Family Treasures

Every once in a while, dedicate a grown-up dinner to a family member who is no longer with you. Use some photos as the centerpiece, put some favorite recipes on the menu, and encourage storytelling geared to your departed loved one. Even if the kids can't add any information, they can participate by listening, and hopefully some of the details of the evening will remain in their hearts.

Collecting Collections

It's not difficult to start a collection—more than two objects of any one thing will do! So why not help your kids start a collection—one that they can display and be responsible for. Now we're not talking Picasso here or antique teddy bears. It can be something as simple as quarters with state names on them, shiny pennies, old keys, or that old standby—stamps. This is a great way to collect some fun moments.

Wrap
and Roll

I know you were kind of busy laboring on the day your kids were born, but it's very easy to get a copy of a newspaper corresponding to the birthdays of your children. Just go to **www.nytimes.com** and order a copy! Once you receive it, copy the pages that your child would find most interesting—sports, comics, or news from the day they entered the world. Now enlarge your photocopies and use them as wrapping paper for birthday presents! It's really not a lot of work. It's a project you can amortize, cuz you'll use this every year.

Sniffle
Suit

Kids have soccer suits and scout suits and softball suits and sailing suits and ski suits, but not every kid has a "sniffle suit." When your little one is under the weather with a tummy ache or a cough and cold, specify a pair of pj's that will forevermore be known as the sniffle suit. These are the pajamas that have the power to send the germ bugs away. This little tradition (along with lots of fluids and the appropriate medicine) will become part of a "get-well" tradition.

Healing the Ultimate Boo-Boo

Nothing stings more than when your kid's feelings are hurt. At that moment, when their whole world has shut down, even the hugest hug in the world doesn't always work. What *does* do the trick is putting a Band-Aid over your little one's heart. After a couple of times, they'll realize that feelings heal just like scrapes and bruises. And when the fog lifts and the smile returns, off comes the Band-Aid. It's a ritual that this big kid still feels like doing.

It's Personal Pizza Time

This is what I was talkin' about in the Intro a few pages back. You never want to stifle creativity, so just let your mini-chefs cook on all four "creativity burners." Buy an empty pizza shell and let your junior Julia Child(ren) concoct any combination of toppings they want. The last time I did this, Cocoa Puffs, mini-marshmallows, hot dogs, red M&M's, and frozen waffle pieces graced the top of the pizza. Don't worry—you only have to *look* at it.

Pizza Perfect

During an interview with Jonathan Lipnicki, the young star of the films *Jerry Maguire* and *Stuart Little* (and one of the cutest little actors on the planet), we started talking about school. Now let's keep in mind that Jonathan is a great student . . . yet when I asked him what he's going to major in, he said, "Pizza!"

I realized that this is a creative concept that can also be a learning tool. For example the concept of fractions can seem very remote for a kid until you bring him down to Mario's on a Saturday afternoon. With the pepperoni pizza in front of you, cut the pie down the center to create two equal halves. Now cut one half in half, and he'll understand what one quarter is (not enough to fill you up!). You can go on and on with this lesson until you get a bellyache, but the knowledge of fractions will be forever etched in your child's stomach lining.

Open Bar

Recently, after a family party, I asked my niece if she'd had a good time and found her response so interesting. She said, "I did, but I don't understand why all the grownups huddle around the drink place. They must be so thirsty. I wish *we* had a drink place."

Now, I assure you that it was not a frozen margarita she was after—she just wanted a place of her own. For our next little shindig, I set up a juice and soda bar for the kids on a low table. I included some kid-friendly snacks, and they had a ball—kind of like playing dress-up!

It's Easy Being Green

Kids are in awe of what they perceive to be "magic." Place a magic spell over any situation and you will have their instant attention.

For a while, it was difficult to get my sleepyhead nephew out of bed in the morning . . . until he discovered that a "magic spell" had been placed over his breakfast. His magical mom was in the kitchen, placing five drops of green food coloring in his juice, as well as the waffle mix. From then on, he would pop out of bed and zoom downstairs to check out whether or not he was going to have eggs abracadabra. Now that he's in the eighth grade, he won't drink green juice anymore—but it was fun while it lasted!

The Learning Menu

When I was young and realized that I was never going to be a math scholar, I kept asking my mom the same old whiny question: "But when am I ever gonna use algebra in the *real* world?" I received the response: "One day it will take you by surprise and you'll really be able to use it, so go back to your room and study."

To this day, 40 zillion years later, I have never used algebra! But putting that aside for a sec, Mom had a wonderful way of taking what we were learning in school and incorporating it into daily life. When we were studying money, making change, and figuring out percentages for gratuities, Mom turned our dining room into a restaurant. Using play money, she'd have us order our breakfast, pay up front, and leave an appropriate tip. It was a terrific way to apply practical knowledge. Years later, Mom played this game with a grandchild who actually brought a credit card to the table! No, she didn't accept it.

Now to this day, if I go out with a big group, I'm the first one to figure out the check breakdown.

Splish-Splash

The writing is on the wall. Most kids don't like bathtime unless they're being entertained while in the tub. And that's fine when you have time, but sometimes you're busy with your 10 zillion, 342 thousand other chores, and the most you can muster up is, "Lynnie, time to scrub-a-dub-dub."

Well, there *is* an item sold at most large superstores that kids absolutely adore. They're soap pens. These little wonders come in every color and actually have the ability to write on bathroom tile, tubs, and faucets . . . until your little devil splashes it all off! If your tiny one can't read, the soap pens can be used for drawing as well. You can also give the pen to your baby bathers and have them create masterpieces while they're in the tub. We've come a long way from rubber duckies!

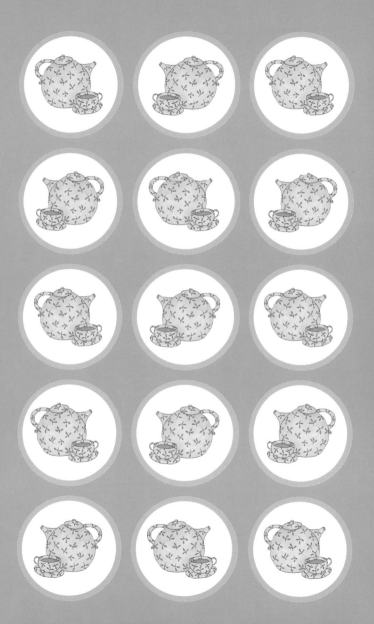

Home is where the heart is. It's also where the clutter collects, the weeds wilt, and the boiler breaks! Now, I'm not trying to sound like Erma Bombeck—I'm much too idealistic for that. I'm just trying to find a happy medium between the pages of *House Beautiful* and reality!

Each month, like clockwork, I devour all of my design magazines, wishing I could just superimpose my little family on the pictures and live on page 22. Then the phone rings, I snap out of my wishful thinking, and I do some *creative* thinking.

Of course we can't all just open up our checkbooks and decide to remodel the kitchen, add a kids' wing, and put a fireplace and French doors in the master bedroom so we can gaze upon the new limestone pool and tennis courts. (This whole fantasy was brought to you from a gal who lives in a two-bedroom apartment!) But every day, we *can* be our own contractors by sprinkling some magic into our homes and adding . . . (you guessed it!) those little touches.

Petal Power

One of nature's little miracles is a rose. It actually takes 56 days for one to form, then we pick them, worship them, and before we can say, "1-800-FLOWERS," they're gone. But there are some very easy "petal projects" that can elongate their lives.

Homemade rose water can be used as a refreshing toner. It also makes a lovely gift (I don't often use the word *lovely*, but this *is* lovely). Simply mix 1/2 cup of rose petals with a pint of spring water. Add one teaspoon of glycerin or baby oil and 1/2 cup of alcohol. Place it in the fridge and shake daily for 14 days. After two weeks, you can store it anywhere.

Rose water is also a sweet sealant for envelopes. Just dab some on a cotton puff and place it on the glue of the envelope—I even do it on my AmEx bill, with hopes that they won't cash my checks!

You can also dip some washcloths into the rose water, squeeze out the excess moisture, roll them up, and store them in the fridge. They become a unique way to wipe off your hands during a greasy dinner party, and they're great for joggers when they return home from their run.

Pillow Talk

What a cute movie . . . but never mind, that's not what we're supposed to be talking about. Okay, I've never understood the concept of splurging on a party dress (that you may wear three or four times a year), yet you're tightening your belt when it comes to your sleeping partner (no, I'm not getting personal). I'm talking about your pillow. A survey was done stating that on average, people keep their pillows for ten years or more. A lot of people don't even keep their spouses for that long! But unless you're an insomniac, you spend about 50 hours a week with your puffy pal . . . and if you haven't shopped for a new one in recent years, you're missing out on a dreamy experience! Amortize your purchase over each use, and what a deal! Pleasant dreams!

Landscaping
Legacies

Whenever a child is born in your inner circle, plant a brand-new tree in their honor and place it in the front yard of your home. So if you move, the child will always be able to look at the "legacy" from the street. They will both grow together and share a lifetime. If you don't have a front lawn, permanently borrow a spot from a loved one. I promise you, they won't say no.

Instant Renovation

I would love to rip down my bathroom walls, gut the whole room, put in a Jacuzzi, and add beautiful French tile, but since I don't have the time or the trust fund, I decided to renovate the "little things." To give me a sense of freshness and luxury, I chose a brand new accent color and bought fluffy bath mats and shower curtains in the new hue.

Next, I kicked my products up a notch. French milled lavender soap in a provincial limestone dish is much more cost efficient than retiling the whole kit-and-caboodle. A brand new high-tech toothbrush is next, as well as a couple of new magazine subscriptions for bathroom reading.

Brrrr!

There's nothing like a family gathering around the fireplace to take the chill out of the winter air. But just because you don't have a fireplace doesn't mean you have to miss out on all the cool accessories. With a little imagination, some cardboard, and a marker, you won't even notice the difference.

Take a large piece of cardboard and draw the best possible fireplace that you can. Don't worry — this isn't going to hang in a museum. You just need a sketched image. Lean it against the wall where a hearth might have gone. Stir up some creamy hot chocolate, and make some gooey s'mores. Who could ask for a cozier evening in front of the "fire"?!

Trimming a Tree for All Seasons

So much time, effort, and love goes into decorating a Christmas tree, but when the ornaments go back into hibernation, it creates such a void in the home. So why not get a little artificial tree and let your kids decorate it for each season and family occasion: birthdays, Halloween, anniversaries, springtime, graduation—and even Columbus Day. It's a great family activity and doesn't even need watering!

Heavenly
Secrets

The Manele Bay Hotel in Lanai, Hawaii, is way beyond heavenly. The good news is that some of the pampered perks they provide are easy for you to do for yourself in your own little piece of heaven. For example, when the winds of winter start knocking at your door, drying and chafing every body part in sight, keep your skin moist by warming up your moisturizer in the microwave. A 60-second zap also adds coziness to your massage oil, lip salves, socks, and even pillowcases!

Conversely, keeping astringent, day cream, or toners in the fridge during hot, steamy weather is refreshing and therapeutic. I've also put pillowcases in the freezer. Not only will they keep you cool on a balmy August night, they take up so much room that you won't be able to squeeze in that pint of Häagen-Dazs. So you'll be cool *and* thin!

Here's an Idea

(picture a lightbulb going off)

Restaurant design consultants often suggest the color red for dining rooms. It stimulates the appetite, aids in digestion (and adds to the bill). The color blue is often used in medical waiting rooms for its calming effect. And yellow can often be seen in classrooms, as it's supposed to help keep students awake. If you don't want to paint, paper, and redesign your room, but want to reap the advantages of using these colors, you can do it with light. Simply install some colored bulbs in each room until you reach the desired effect. If you can't find colored lightbulbs in your hometown hardware store, or you don't want to make the investment, you can also use gels. This is cellophane-coated paper that fits over your regular bulbs which will offer you the same effect. You can try green bulbs when you're making investments, but I don't think it will work!

Dream
Home

It may be the case that I never get to live in my ultimate dream house. I've done everything possible to create magical residences, but I still can't see the ocean when I wake up, or a mountain sunset at dusk.

Oh, but I *can*, actually—I just can't live there! You see, I keep an album in my bedroom that contains every homey picture that has ever given me the chills or caused me to say "Ahhhh." Years and years of magazine cut-outs that tickle my aesthetic bones fill those pages.

Sure, it would be sweet if we could all live our dreams, but looking at these dreamy images brings me pleasure every time. Why don't you try it?

Good Scents

Aromas jolt the senses and inspire the soul. Beyond potpourri and air fresheners, there are other ways to bring home the sweet smell of success. . . . Place a few drops of your favorite perfume on a cotton ball and dab it on your lightbulbs. Then, every time you turn them on, they will heat the oil in the perfume. . . . Sprinkle some dried lavender or scented powder in your pillowcases for a relaxing sleep. . . . And if Rover has missed his designated target over and over again, just simmer two tablespoons each of vanilla and cinnamon extract in a cup of water. It will neutralize pet accidents.

Dishwashing Diva

Did you ever count up the number of hours you've washed dishes in your lifetime? (I haven't either—it would be a foolish waste of time.) Anyway, the answer is probably "A lot." So since I spend so much time in the vicinity of the kitchen sink, I like to surround myself with a little eye candy. I pour my dishwashing liquid into a fabulous flea-market find—a glass vial with a universal pour stop. It can make this tedious daily ritual much more pleasant!

Second-Aid Box

First-aid boxes help people in medical emergencies. "Second-aid" boxes answer the call of life's *little* emergencies. Create a box with universal items in it—ones that you may not necessarily use but that solve immediate problems: temporary dental glue; beige stockings in S, M, and L; contact lens cleaner; a prepaid FedEx slip; travelers' checks; and generic reading glasses. Put the box in a back closet until a guest in your home is in dire need of a second-aid box! Since I obviously don't know your buddies, it's hard for me to suggest how you should customize your box. But just put in everything under the sun, and you'll be prepared for any nonmedical emergency.

Let There Be Light

Even if the view from your bedroom windows is of a red brick wall, let there be light. At least once a month, lift those blinds, pull those curtains, and open all of the windows as wide as possible. Let your home take a big nourishing in-breath and out-breath!

Sew, a Needle Pulling Thread

I find that some of my favorite things are personalized, and if you feel the same way, a quick and easy way to add that oh-so-personal touch to your home can be found at your local tailor. It only takes a few minutes to monogram sheets, pillows, and fabrics. Your look can range from funky to formal . . . phrases such as "Sleep with the Angels" on your sheets, "No Snoring Sam" on his pillowcase . . . your initials on the backs of your dining room chairs. . . .Why pay through the nose for "status" names and initials? Use your own!

Silent Night

No, I'm not talkin' Christmas here. Conversation over dinner can be delicious, but so can silence. Every now and again, my family and I have a "silent dinner"—zero conversation. No "Please pass the peas" or "What happened at work today?" Just a totally quiet and unique meal where the experience speaks for itself. You'll discover so many little things that by the end of the meal, your dining room will look different to you.

I first tried this at Rancho La Puerta, a perfect spiritual getaway in Tecate, Mexico. I have to admit, I was leery, but because everything that they do there is remarkable, I trusted the Ranch, and as usual, their guidance and nurturing were beyond excellent.

Good Morning, Sunshine!

Re-creating sunlight when your apartment looks out on a graffiti-covered brick wall may not be necessary for survival, but for me, it *is* essential for happiness. Instead of turning my whole apartment building around (which would be a mean feat), I just buy some full-spectrum lightbulbs at the hardware store—they actually mimic sunlight—and they'll sure brighten up all your days!

The Ultimate Bedspread

It was faux fur in the '80s, sensual silk in the '90s, and nature's own in the new century: personalized bedspreads with your initials, a design, or a phrase spelled out in flowers. You don't have to be artistic to do this—you just can't be allergic to flowers!

Okay, make sure your bedspread is pulled taut. Take a piece of scrap paper and sketch out the oversized initials you want to use. Then simply sprinkle flower petals or leaves on the bed to create your design. If it's a child's bed, it's fun to do a happy-face design. And if you don't have the time to place your petals in specific spots, just sprinkle them all over the place and put your petal to the metal.

Spring Cleaning

ey, there's too much to do in the spring. I suggest we move this ritual to the winter. You don't really need the great outdoors to clean underneath the box spring or go through the stacked boxes in the attic. If you spread the Big Kahuna tasks over all the seasons, they won't even seem like such a big deal. A logical thing . . . yet a little one.

Can
We
Dish?

So the boss's wife (who hasn't smiled since the Civil War) comes over to your home for dinner and is regaled with your beautiful china, your very best silverware, and (good gracious!) cloth napkins . . . while the very next night, your wonderful family eats chipped beef off of chipped plates.

You don't *have to* save the good stuff for special occasions, you know. Your family members are the most special guests you'll ever have. And if a fancy-schmancy plate gets broken, you can call **1-800-REPLACE** to replace your china for a reasonable price.

Good Golly Gardenias

For centuries, poets have written about the fleeting beauty of flowers. I've often wondered why weeds last forever, yet my precious petals have such a short life span. Naturally, when you cut their stems on a slant underwater—ensuring that no air bubbles travel up the stem—their life expectancy goes up about 45 percent, but in my book, it's still too short. One of my favorite flowers is the glorious gardenia. It's a stubborn plant—it doesn't like to be moved and likes to be thirsty and dry at the same time (go figure). But when that winsome white bud appears unexpectedly on the branch, it's time for celebration!

Cutting the flower right underneath the last petals and floating it in a clear glass bowl can change the whole atmosphere of a room. It's a simple and spectacular statement for your eyes and your nose. There's only one problem: The joy is fleeting, since the gardenia wilts so quickly. I'm always an advocate for all live plants and flowers to oxygenate the air and to rejuvenate the soul. But here's one little artificial idea that works wonders: Find two or three pretty plastic gardenias and spray them lightly with gardenia essence oil. Then float away! Fake, yes, but so is Disneyland!

Finders
Keepers

Because I'm a flea-market junkie (which you've probably guessed), I've collected boxes and boxes of junk jewelry throughout the years. But just because the average price of my jewels is about five bucks, it doesn't mean that I don't treasure these . . . treasures.

When you have a lot of stuff, it's hard to organize it all—how do you find that clunky silver necklace when you actually need it?! Now I can find any of my sparkling junk within a split second, thanks to a plastic hanging shoetree. It's about $24 in most hardware stores and provides a great system to store jewelry. Simply slip your gems into each plastic slot, organized by color or type. Because the shoe hanger is transparent, your 14-carat needs are met instantly!

Changing Tables

I have a love/hate relationship with e-mail. I adore the instant communication, but I miss the personal contact. More and more each day, we're becoming known by our log-ins, our cell phone numbers, and our computer addresses.

To counterbalance the world we live in, I try to personalize life whenever I can. Here's something I did recently for a birthday celebration, and I could have opened a small business with all the interest it garnered.

Just find an old, beat-up table at the flea market, or even in your own basement. Spray-paint it in one solid color. Using stencils and masking tape, think of a name or phrase that you'd like to transfer to the side or tabletop. Line up your stencils and tape it to the table. Use newspaper to protect the rest of the table's surface. Spray-paint the stencil using a different color from the table, and peel it off gently. I wrote "Danny's Delicious Desserts," and used my new masterpiece as a buffet table for my birthday boy's birthday cake and other sensational sweets. Danny loved this sooooo much that I gave him the table, but you can also spray-paint over your letters and use this idea again for another occasion.

Fits to a Tee

When I was little (and big) I collected everything—I called it "art"—but my grandma called it "junk." However, one collection I was extremely attached to was composed of my T-shirts. Due to lack of space, I proudly displayed them in a back drawer until the day my magical mom came up with an ingenious idea that I still use today as a creative flare in a kid's room.

She used my collection as curtains. Yes, curtains. Okay, I'll explain. She wound a clothesline around the curtain pole, and using clothespins, hung some shirts across the windows. It's really adorable and only takes about ten minutes. I've also done this with different colors of kid's jeans. It may sound like I'm hangin' my ideas out to dry, but this is really curtain-raising.

Split-Second Centerpieces

Some of my favorite three-word phrases are: "I love you" (that's a given), "baked on premises," and "last-minute company." That's right, last-minute company is nothing to get the sweats over. You may not be able to serve your favorite slow-roasted turkey, but everything will be fine as long as you do a little creative thinking. One thing you won't have time to do is run out to your flower shop, but it's quick and easy to put together a split-second centerpiece without the perfect petals.

First of all, think of the hobbies and interests your guests of honor enjoy. If they love boating, go to your kid's bathroom, take that plastic boat, and plop it on a blue napkin in the center of your table. That should float their boat! If they're tennis players, take a couple of balls, write your menu on them in permanent marker, and you're all "set." A match made in creative heaven. And if you need a more sophisticated look, somewhere in your home there's a small mirror. Take it off the wall and place it face-up in the center of your table. Place your pretty wine glasses on it, and it will reflect your warm welcome. The centerpiece of entertaining is your spirit—and your little creative touches.

Warehouse Woes

I adore warehouse shopping. It saves me tons of moolah and time. But, unless you happen to live in an airplane hangar, what do you do with 20 rolls of paper towels and toilet paper?

Well, Queen Elizabeth may not do this at Buckingham Palace, but I actually use these rolls as a temporary storage table base. I line them up evenly, stick a shelf or piece of cardboard on top of the paper goods, and use this little table until it's time to go back to the warehouse.

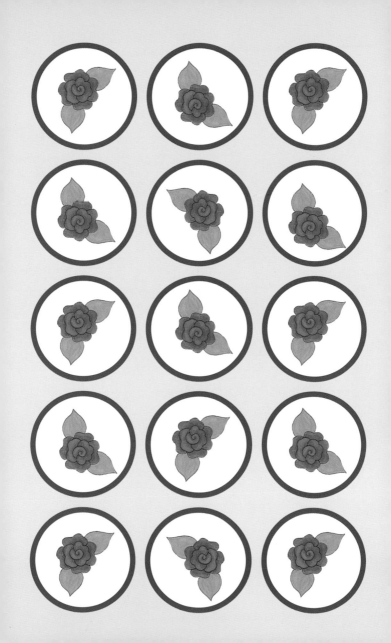

Honey—it glistens and shines and naturally sweetens everything in its path. And once it touches you, it's hard not to accept. I just love the word *honey* and all that it represents. It always reminds me that when you add just a couple drops of kindness and sweetness into the mix, it can instantly change the flavor of your situation.

At the very beginning of a relationship—when both of you are still absolutely perfect and no one is leaving the cap off the toothpaste—it seems to take so little effort to do nice, nurturing things for one another. And then gradually, real life sets in and one of the first things to fly out the window is all that special stuff you used to do for each other.

Well, healthy, happy relationships are not about sweeping each other off your feet every time that you walk into the room. It's about making sure that you "dust" on a daily basis. And just in case your creative juices have gotten a little dusty, this chapter is chock-ful of all those little things that can make a real difference for you and your honey!

Royal Relationships

If given the choice, I would never want to be in the shoes of Queen Elizabeth of England. But if I were, I would certainly choose a pair of strappy sandals. But all of us should be treated like a king or queen in our kingdom. Naturally, that might interfere with changing the diapers, doing the laundry, and driving the carpool, but not if you plan your court. Set aside a night every once in a while to be king or queen for a day. From your favorite foods to your favorite hobby to control of the remote control, it's your day to rule!

C'mon Baby, Light My Fire

Nothin' like the sound of breaking waves or the crackling of a fire to add to your R&R (Relationship & Romance)! Although I believe in miracles, I have a weak lower back, so I simply don't have the power to move your home to an ocean-front location—but I *can* tell you about an incredible CD that can audibly turn your plain-Jane Sheetrock into a ski lodge in Gstaad! Just log on to **www.firesoundscd.com,** and for about $15.99, you can change the atmosphere of your entire evening.

Time Out

No matter how wild your four-year-old gets, you know that "time-out" will really stop him in his tracks. Sometimes some 40-year-olds need to be stopped in their tracks, too! You and your partner should think of a word or signal that each of you can use to stop the action during a heated discussion . . . before things escalate and get out of hand. It's always a good idea to take a time-out—no matter how old you are!

Vacant
Vacation

When I start to drool as I flip through magazines and see couples romping on a magnificent beach, I know the reason. I'm certainly not salivating for the hunk in the picture, or envious of the model's thighs (okay, maybe just a little). I'm drooling because it's vacation time. But just knowing what time it is doesn't mean you can necessarily act on your desires.

No time or money for two weeks in Maui? Then bring Maui to you! "Mini-vacations" that break up the predictability of life are easy, fun, and even therapeutic. All it takes is some creativity and a willing mate who doesn't think you're crazy.

I changed into my 12-year-old faded Hawaiian shirt, moved my garden to the center of the table, whipped up some piña coladas and served them in pineapple shells, played some Don Ho music in the CD player, put some plastic flowers in my hair, and set up a fan at the edge of the dining room to simulate a gentle Pacific breeze. Authentic? No way. Fun? Absolutely.

You could also travel to Paris, Rome, Athens, or Nairobi for the night. You won't get any frequent-flyer miles, but you won't get jet lag either!

Eiffel Tower Envy

One of my dreams is to wake up every day with the sun reflecting off the Eiffel Tower—so naturally, in the interim, I've put a three-inch replica on my nightstand. When my honey and I are lucky enough to be in the City of Lights, we turn the town inside out, touring everything in sight and soaking up all of the "Parisian Factoids" that we can absorb.

But whether you hang your shingle 15 miles outside of the South of France or South Dakota, every town is interesting in its own way. So, every once in a while, be a tourist in your own hometown, cameras and all. Set aside a Sunday to view your Main Street as you've never seen it before. (I'm a little ashamed to admit that I lived in New York for almost 12 years before I ventured to the top of the Empire State Building or landed near our Lady Liberty.)

Even though my Main Street may have a few more options than yours, looking at your town through different eyes will bring many wonderful things into focus.

Comfort Food and Fashion

Sure, it's fun to get all dressed up, go out on the town, and dance the night away! But to me, there's nothing better than having a true comfy-cozy night at home . . . a pajama party for two. Put on your flannel pj's, take the large cushions off your couch, and plump them up on the carpet to create a pillowed playpen for dinner. Serve macaroni and cheese, chicken potpie—all the comfort food you can muster up. Glamour is great, but comfort is key.

15 Minutes of Fame

While 15 minutes may not seem like a lot of time, it is . . . if you add it to the beginning of your day. Make a deal with your partner that you'll both wake up 15 minutes earlier than usual. It won't affect your beauty sleep, but this gift of time can affect your life. By now, we all have our morning routines down to the wire, so adding this extra time will seem like such a "little" luxury.

Child's Play

Don't ever act like a baby, but keep the "child" inside of your relationship alive by playing with each other. We spend so much time talking about the mortgage, Danny's second-grade teacher, and Mom's living arrangement that we lose sight of the fun. So go out and play! It doesn't have to cost you anything, and the payback is remarkable. You can play board games on Sunday, go to the swings in the park, or play *Jeopardy* along with the TV show . . . and play for points (even though you both will be winners)!

Sometimes in a relationship, one of the partners has an inner child roaming inside of them, but the other is a pure, unadulterated adult. But this doesn't mean that you shouldn't go out and play. Remember, playmates don't have to be the same age!

Happy Multi-Anniversary

Besides Ben & Jerry's Chunky Monkey, I think rituals—those repeated behaviors that bond you to people and to your personal history—are the glue of life. Here's one that I've borrowed from my friends Jen and Jason, and I'm never gonna return it.

They met on June 22nd, and then married on the same date two years later. They not only celebrate their wedding anniversary, but set aside the "22nd of every month as their sacred day. The pair will not let anything stand in their way of sharing their "22" night. It's a wonderful way to keep kindling the spark, to nurture the relationship, and to keep current on first-run movies.

If you're not able to carve out one night a month, any commitment will do. Just plan it far enough in advance and stick to the sked!

Sweet Smell of Success

I've been wearing Shalimar since Abe Lincoln was in diapers. . . . okay, a slight exaggeration, but I've been wearing it for so long that I can't even smell it on myself anymore. But my man can, and he loves it. So when he goes on a business trip "solo," I put a few drops of Shalimar on a piece of cotton, wrap it in foil, and place it in an unsuspecting spot in his luggage or briefcase. Once he found it in the middle of a presentation . . . and he got the account!

Now this is not a commercial endorsement for Shalimar—it's an endorsement to reinforce our senses. A smell can instantly jolt our subconscious and bring up a whole slew of memories.

When I'm away on a business trip without my honey and find myself in a department store (okay, I know I should be working, but everyone needs a break), I mosey on over to the cologne counter and sniff away.

The Complaint Department

Nobody's perfect . . . not even—be still my heart—Brad Pitt. But there *is* a time and a place to vent your complaints so that your defense mechanisms don't switch into overdrive. In our house, my fiancé and I use an egg timer for our gripes and a finite amount of time to speak our respective pieces. We both work very hard to stick to the plan, which is not always easy in the heat of the moment. You have to erase "and just one more thing . . ." from your phraseology.

Now the finite amount of time doesn't include talking through issues. It's a simple idea to make sure you don't keep repeating what the other person has already heard the first time.

Ya Gotta Have Heart

The heart is the ultimate symbol of love—something that we all desire. Even the card industry makes 23 percent of their profits yearly on Valentine's Day! I think V-Day should be celebrated 365 days a year . . . expressing love to your honey, your family, and your friends.

One little tool that comes in very handy is a heart-shaped cookie cutter. It can provide those unexpected moments. I use it to cut carrots, croutons, sandwiches, zucchini, cheese, angel food cake, brownies, croutons—any edible that's shapeable! I don't wear my heart on my sleeve . . . I wear it in the kitchen.

I Miss Mistletoe

There are certain "rules" of life that I just don't understand. For instance, why can't we wear white shoes after Labor Day? Why do you drive on the left in England and the right in America—this just doesn't make any sense to me.

And here's one more. Mistletoe—why just once a year? It's such a welcoming, fun tradition. I put on my investigative journalist hat and found out that it's grown all year long. So I'm going to take a stand, and leave it up in my home for the entire year. I'm also going to take little cuttings and include little pieces of the "pucker-up plant" in cards and letters when appropriate. What a rebel I am!

(But just a side note for you animal lovers— mistletoe's toxic to your little furry critters if ingested, so make sure they keep their paws off of it!)

Step-In Out

I know that by the time you get the baby-sitter, drive 45 minutes to the restaurant, take Fido to the neighbors, and pay the $25 cover charge . . . you realize with your hectic schedules that you're really too pooped to go out. Well, you can go out by staying in, and you don't even have to make a whole night out of it.

For more than 40 years of marriage, my friends June and Dale Von Ruden have been asking each other to dance. Music has always been a backdrop in their home, and they have a tradition of extending their hands to each other for a dance at totally random times. Slow dancing is such an intimate, loving expression . . . one that we don't do enough of because we think that we need all of the appropriate accessories to go with it, but we don't! And you don't even have to dance the night away. You can do it on your way to make dinner. Just put on Sinatra and extend a hand!

Symbolism

By now, I know you've realized that good things come in small packages! If you can't afford that sparkler when you propose to her, or that magnificent 50th wedding anniversary present for your grandparents, or a new computer for your daughter who's starting college—then substitute feelings for your credit card. Think about the sentiment you want to convey, and get something inexpensive that will warm their heart.

For example, maybe . . . a globe with a ribbon around it, with a note that states, "You mean the world to me" . . . 50 candy kisses to represent all the years you were married . . . a childhood birthday photo placed in a beautiful frame—you get the idea. Obviously, gifts don't have to cost big money to make big statements.

Throughout the years, I've received some very extravagant gifts. I'm not saying that I packed them up and handed them back to the gift-giver, but the presents I most remember and cherish were the little ones, such as: (1) A bar of soap from my brother—no, it wasn't a hint that I should bathe more often—it was for helping him out during some hard times. His message was, "Thank you so much for keeping me afloat." (2) A picture of a beautiful necklace that I had been drooling over, folded and placed in a jewelry box with an IOU that simply said, "Someday!" (3) After a motivational speech about "finding your own star power," a member of the audience sent me those sparklers that you put on your birthday cake with a note that said, "You sparkled!"

Just remember: It's easy to exchange big thoughts with little things.

The Workplace

Those Seven Dwarfs were onto something when they belted out their hit number "Whistle While You Work." As Snow White looked on, melodic wisdom flowed out of the mouths of these little men. Happy, Dopey, and the rest of the gang knew that life at work can often resemble a fairy tale if you have the right attitude.

A lot of people I know sing "The Sunday Night Blues," realizing that on Monday morning they'll be back at the ol' office. There's nothing I can do to help you change your job, but I *can* help you make some little changes that can help you out in the workplace. They may not mirror the environment that your brother-in-law toils in—ya know, the barefoot one who works in his pajamas from his deck overlooking the Mediterranean—but every little bit helps.

Naturally, you'll have to work within your corporate culture, but there are some creative comfort kernels in this chapter that no one needs to know about except you.

It's our little secret . . . so start whistling!

Just
Do It!

I don't mean to sound like an ad for Nike, but in the workplace, those three words say it all. It's Monday morning, you come in all relaxed from a wonderful weekend, and then you realize that there are three rather unpleasant calls that you have to make. Instead of procrastinating and allowing the gray-cloud feeling to float over you all day, *just do it!* Get the most difficult things out of the way first, so they don't chip away at your energy. (This relates to my dentist theory, which says: *Always schedule a root canal at 8 A.M., never at 4 P.M. It will weigh you down all day long.*)

Escape Hatch

Whether you're in a plush corner office with a view, or a windowless basement cubicle, make sure you provide an escape hatch for yourself at work by creating a mini photo display in your area. Of course, family pix will probably be front and center, but be sure to also include some pictures of places that can momentarily transport you—the beach in Maui, that apricot-colored rosebush in the park—these are images that can instantly release tension and relax your spirit.

The Clean Machine

At home, I'm a human clean machine—even my trash cans shine! Unfortunately, my office is a disaster. A couple of years ago, I was doing an article for *Cosmopolitan,* and they came to shoot a layout of me behind my desk. The only problem was . . . they couldn't find it!

You see, what *I* could never find was the time to clean it. But I discovered a little solution that may not be featured in any magazine, but which has definitely helped. I know you certainly don't have a half hour to stop what you're doing and clean off your desk either . . . but if you devote just six minutes at the end of each day to this task, you've just done your half-hour's worth by week's end (and you might also find those papers you were looking for).

Be a Drip

Candles are no longer reserved for romance. Not only do they set the mood, but they can also *change* the mood. They're therapeutic and can create an ambiance of serenity, energy, mental clarity, and strength.

These melting miracles also opened up a certain TV anchor's air passages when she had the flu with a 102-degree fever. You've heard the expression "The show must go on"? Well, they're not exaggerating. There I was, a total drip, about to interview Sophia Loren, when a savior in the next office lit a eucalyptus candle. It was even better than cold medicine because I could still operate heavy machinery! I know some offices don't allow employees to burn candles, but if yours does, you can really wax poetic in their wake!

You're "It"!

In the office game of business "tag," professional responsibilities change hands daily. To enhance your 9 to 5 office life, continue the game of tag by taking turns nurturing each other. Alternate the task of bringing in delicious lunches, nourishing beverages, and fresh flowers for your little group. It's very time-consuming doing this for yourself on a daily basis, but if you're "it" and only have to be responsible for these things a few times a month, it's much more manageable. Just don't play hide-and-seek with the good stuff.

The Fantastics

Whenever you asked my grandma, "How are you doing?" she would emphatically reply, "Fantastic!" Her answer would make everyone around her feel better. The last time I asked Granny how she was doin', she said, "Wonderful." The amazing thing was . . . she was also on her deathbed and passed away ten minutes later!

Listen to yourself the next time you're asked that question in the workplace. Take yourself off of automatic pilot and answer with a positive affirmation. The people around you will also react positively, and you'll feel great!

Walk the Walk

Most of us are creatures of habit. We take the same route to work every day, listen to the same radio station, and stop at the same coffee bar. It's not a negative trait, it's a secure one, but it may also shut down the avenue of possibilities. So next time you enter your workplace, why not take a different route to your desk. It may seem a tad awkward at first—especially if you don't know a lot of people in the department you're walking through—but once you establish a comfort zone, you'll know them all!

Wheeeeee!

Remember when you were a kid poised at the tippy-top of a swing set, about to start your thrilling downward trajectory? Once the ride started, the only thing you could muster up to shriek was, "Wheeeeee!" Such a joyous sound—and such a powerful word in the workplace.

Learn to be a part of your corporate culture by constantly using the word *we* instead of *I*. Even if you're in an office of just six people, this word will naturally integrate you into the group, and position you as a team player.

Business Trip Treats

You're at the airport and you hear the dreaded announcement, "We're so sorry, but flight 22 has a new departure time of 9:20—please return to the gate area 3½ hours from now." You *could* grab a bite, do a little work, or play games on your laptop—or you could witness one of the most heartwarming aspects of the human condition. Take yourself over to the international arrivals area (believe me, you have plenty of time), and intently study the faces of the people waiting for their loved ones. The body language and facial expressions when the plane's arrival is announced, the anticipation when the passengers disembark, the hugging and kissing that ensues—this is such an uplifting thing to witness!

But make sure you get back to your gate on time . . . or your *own* friends and relatives will miss out on the experience!

Bozo Business

In some industries, wearing a light blue shirt instead of a white one was once considered dressing down. My, my, how times have changed! Now, even my doctor wears a Hawaiian shirt!

Consultants now recognize the importance of fun workplace environments. They've found that laughing and goofing around actually increases productivity. Some corporations even hire clowns, comics, and musicians to tickle funny bones and release pressure. (As a matter of fact, Tiger Woods finds that his most powerful and effective stroke comes into play when he's the most relaxed.) So if your work environment doesn't support these methods, work on them as an individual. Do your part to establish an upbeat, relaxed atmosphere. Maybe they won't call it *work* anymore!

Motivating Melodies

I t's a tie score in the last two minutes of the Super Bowl, so what's the coach to do? Call a time-out right in the thick of things to pump up the players, or say something calming to relax them?

Since *your* boss probably doesn't call a time-out to rev you up or calm you down, *coach yourself* . . . with music. We all have specific songs that energize or relax us. Why not keep those melodies handy in your office and take some mini music breaks when needed. If radios or CD players are frowned upon, take a little walk . . . with your Walkman (or woman). I've even privately serenaded myself in the ladies' room!

Talk the Talk

No matter what biz you're in, a positive, confident outlook is the attitude of choice, but just in case you're feeling a little insecure on the inside, positive affirmations can get you back in shape in no time. Affirmations are really *any* thoughts that you say or think on a regular basis, so you might as well make them positive because . . .when you say them to yourself enough times, they will actually stick in your subconscious and affect your life in multiple ways. At first when I started doing this, I kind of felt like Rainman—but look at him—he won an Oscar!

Comfort Zone

Hopefully, in your office you don't have as many distractions as you do at home. There's no four-year-old pulling at your jacket for apple juice (although your boss does sometimes act like a baby!), and there's no blaring TV noise emanating from the family room. But still . . . sometimes you just can't seem to get the ol' brain to function in that little room at the office, so why not bring the work home.

If a problem you're dealing with is complex and you just can't seem to find a solution, your comfy living room or den might be just the place to crack the code. When everyone is tucked in, put on those well-worn sweats, settle down into your coziest nook and cranny, and revisit the troublesome issue. Oftentimes, being physically relaxed helps to sharpen mental acuity.

Name Game

In this high-tech world of cell-phone numbers, computer codes, and e-mail addresses, it's so important to retain that "personal touch." In business, make sure you address the voice on the other end of the line by name! If calling executives is part of your daily routine, know the names of their assistants, too—they're the gatekeepers.

Even if you're phoning for dinner reservations or seats on the next flight to Chicago, ask the person's name and use it. It creates instant intimacy, instant relationships . . . and instant results!

Elevator Etiquette

I don't get it . . . we silently stand upright in a vertical box, listen to boring music, and stare straight ahead as if we're waiting for a feature film to start.

Why don't people talk in elevators? *I do,* and I've met some fascinating friends along the way. Don't wait until the elevator gets stuck to strike up a conversation. People are much more interesting than illuminated floor numbers.

In with the Good, Out with the Bad

We wake up, stretch, and take a deep breath. Perhaps we work out, go for a walk, and take a deep breath. Then we go eight to ten hours with no time to even *catch* our breath. If we can make time for *latte* breaks, what about *breathing* breaks?.

Just uncross your legs and take some nice, long inhales and exhales throughout the day. In with the good, out with the bad.

Business
Trip 24/7

When you're traveling from city to city, trying to close that really huge deal, you can sometimes lose sight of what city you're in. So force yourself to take a break. No, don't take a nap—find out where the nearest church or temple is located and go and sit in the sanctuary to remind yourself that there's more to life than business. We all know that deep inside . . . but sometimes we just need a little reminder.

For Me?

e can all pick up a dozen carnations from the grocery store, stick 'em in a vase, and add a splash of color to our day, but I love the mysterious moment when the mailroom guy comes around the corner balancing a cellophane-covered flower arrangement. Then, as if in slow motion, it's carried to the desk, and invariably you query, "For me?"

Well, in case this doesn't happen as often as you'd like it to, *make* it happen. That's right—send flowers to yourself every once in a while. Just because Prince or Princess Charming may be on hiatus right now doesn't mean that you shouldn't treat yourself regally! Just make sure to innocently utter the words, "For me?" when they're carried to your desk!

Stay-Well Day

Hey, don't use all your sick days for when you're sick. Prevention is the name of the game. Every once in a while, you need to take a day off to stay well—both mentally and physically. Instead of going to the doc . . . why not go to the dock, the front porch, the park down the street, one of those Disney places . . . just have fun and leave the work environment behind.

Terrific Transfer

At work, we transfer files, we transfer phone calls, we transfer e-mails, we transfer money—that's all well and good for work efficiency, but what about transferring something to make your days more pleasant? At my job, it's difficult to carve out enough time to leave the building to eat lunch, so all of us either order in or eat last night's leftovers.

For the past year, I've been madly in love with The Zone diet, where they deliver divine diet delicacies for each meal. But as I gazed around our lunch area one day, I realized that we were all dining out of plastic microwaveable containers. The next day, we each brought a favorite plate to eat off of. Now, each noon hour, when The Zone people do their thing, I do mine . . . and transfer my lunch to a hand-painted, floral pottery plate. It's such a little thing, but one I wish I'd started dishing out a long time ago!

Okay, you don't get any fabulous parting gifts or $10,000 rebate checks for finishing this book . . . because, as you've probably figured out by now, it's not about the grand gesture! (Although I know the check might have been nice.)

What you *do* get, however, is not only the *knowledge* that "little things make a big difference," but specific ways to put that knowledge to use.

I hope you use these ideas in great health and happiness . . . and spread the good feelings all over the world!

*"I would love to hear from you.
If you have some 'little things' of
your own that you would like
to share, please send me an
e-mail at:* **LaurinSydney@aol.com**. *
It could make a big difference!"*

— **Laurin Sydney**

About the Author

An award-winning journalist, **Laurin Sydney** has anchored television's only live, daily, worldwide entertainment news show on CNN for the past decade. Focusing on the star-studded worlds of film, television, music, and pop culture, she is also a motivational speaker and the author of the critically acclaimed lifestyle book, ***WHY BOTHER? WHY NOT!: A Hollywood Insider Shows You How to Entertain Like a Star, in a Snap!***

Other Hay House Lifestyles Titles of Related Interest

Flip Books

101 Ways to Happiness, by Louise L. Hay
101 Ways to Romance, by Barbara De Angelis, Ph.D.
101 Ways to Transform Your Life,
by Dr. Wayne W. Dyer

Books

Home Design with Feng Shui A–Z,
by Terah Kathryn Collins
The Love and Power Journal, by Lynn V. Andrews
Meditations, by Sylvia Browne
Pleasant Dreams, by Amy E. Dean
Simple Things, by Jim Brickman
You Can Heal Your Life Gift Edition, by Louise L. Hay

Card Decks

Feng Shui Personal Paradise Cards
(booklet and card deck), by Terah Kathryn Collins
Four Agreements Cards, by DON Miguel Ruiz
Heart and Soul, by Sylvia Browne
Inner Peace Cards, by Dr. Wayne W. Dyer
MarsVenus Cards, by John Gray
Power Thoughts for Teens, by Louise L. Hay
Self-Care Cards, by Cheryl Richardson

All of the above titles may be ordered by calling
Hay House at the numbers on the next page.

We hope you enjoyed this Hay House
Lifestyles book. If you would like to receive
a free catalog featuring additional
Hay House books and products, or
if you would like information about the
Hay Foundation, please contact:

Hay House, Inc.
P.O. Box 5100
Carlsbad, CA 92018-5100

(760) 431-7695 or **(800) 654-5126**
(760) 431-6948 (fax) or **(800) 650-5115 (fax)**

Hay House Australia Pty Ltd
P.O. Box 515
Brighton-Le-Sands, NSW 2216
phone: 1800 023 516
e-mail: info@hayhouse.com.au

Please visit the Hay House Website at: **hayhouse.com**